Learn a Language!

See and Say
German

by Monika Estrada

CAPSTONE PRESS
a capstone imprint

Published by Pebble, an imprint of Capstone
1710 Roe Crest Drive, North Mankato, Minnesota 56003
capstonepub.com

Library of Congress Cataloging-in-Publication Data is available on the Library of Congress website.

ISBN: 9780756581770 (hardcover)
ISBN: 9780756581862 (paperback)
ISBN: 9780756581817 (ebook PDF)

Summary: How do you tell someone that you're hungry in German? What's the German word for *airplane*? With this book, curious kids will see and say simple words and phrases in German.

Editorial Credits
Editor: Ericka Smith; Designer: Sarah Bennett; Media Researcher: Svetlana Zhurkin; Production Specialist: Katy LaVigne

Image Credits
Getty Images: Adam Berry, 27 (bottom), Allan Baxter, 18 (bottom right), Arx0nt, 5 (middle right), 11 (top right), Deagreez, 17 (bottom), FamVeld, 23 (top right), IGphotography, 15 (bottom), Luis Alvarez, 14 (bottom), Maskot, 6, 18 (bottom left), querbeet, 25 (bottom left), ridvan_celik, 22 (bottom), romrodinka, 16 (bottom), Rossella De Berti, 14 (top), Ryan McVay, 16 (top), Simon Ritzmann, 19 (bottom left), solidcolours, 7 (bottom left), Stock4B-RF/Carlos Hernandez, 9 (top), Westend61, 7 (top), 8; Shutterstock: Alexey YanLev, 23 (bottom left), Aliaksei Hintau, 13 (middle right), Anna Titova, 12 (top left), Annabell Gsoedl, 12 (bottom right), asife, 31 (middle), bergamont, 29 (middle right), Bjoern Wylezich, 20 (top and middle), Boonchuay Promjiam, 29 (bottom left), Clara Bastian, cover (middle left), David C. Rehner, cover (bottom left), Dmitrij Skorobogatov, cover (top right), Elena Berd, 21 (top), Elizabeth_0102, 29 (middle left), elxeneize, 18 (top right), Eric Isselee, 13 (middle left), FamVeld, 30 (middle left), Fascinadora, 30 (middle), footageclips, 27 (top right), FooTToo, 13 (bottom), Fotofermer, 28 (bottom left), Frank Fischbach, 25 (top left), GK1982, 15 (middle), gofra, 26 (middle left), halimqd (speech bubble and burst), cover and throughout, Here, 5 (top), 23 (top left), HighKey, 17 (top), imageBROKER, 13 (top right), industryviews, 21 (middle left), Irina Wilhauk, 31 (top), J2R, 4, Janna Danilova, 10 (left), Jinga, 17 (middle), Joan Carles Juarez, 13 (top left), Juergen Faelchle, 27 (top left), Karl Allgaeuer, 11 (top left), Krakenimages, 7 (bottom right), Ljupco Smokovski, 23 (bottom right), LP Design, 12 (top right), Lukassek, 19 (top left), Magnia (lined texture), cover and throughout, Majonit, 5 (middle left), 25 (top right), Maks Narodenko, 11 (bottom left), Markus Mainka, 20 (bottom), Michael Shake, 21 (bottom), Mickis-Fotowelt, 26 (middle right), Mo Photography Berlin, 19 (top right), Mohamed 28, 21 (middle right), Naypong Studio, 29 (top), New Africa, cover (top left), nukeaf, 24, oksana2010, 12 (bottom left), 28 (top right), Olha Rohulya, 26 (bottom), Pani Garmyder, 19 (bottom right), phaustov, 18 (middle), pikselstock, 9 (bottom), Pixel-Shot, 15 (top), 22 (middle left), Roman Samborskyi, cover (bottom right), 1, Ruth Black, 30 (top, middle right, and bottom), 31 (middle right, middle left, and bottom), SeventyFour, 22 (middle right), spiharu.u (spot line art), cover and throughout, Stepanek Photography, 10 (right), Tim UR, 11 (bottom right), Traveller70, 18 (top left), Vangert, 28 (bottom right), Vitalii Stock, 7 (middle), William Perugini, 19 (middle), winphong, 29 (bottom right), wu hsoung, 25 (bottom right)

Printed and bound in China. PO5834

Table of Contents

The German Language

The German language that most people speak today comes from a form of the language that dates back to the sixth century. German is now an official language in six European countries. Some estimate that for about 90 million people, German is their first language.

An official language is a language that many people in a country speak. It might be used by the government, at schools, and in other important places.

How to Use This Book

Some words and phrases complete a sentence.
Those will appear in bold.

`English` **I like . . .**

`German` Ich mag . . .

`Say It!` 🐱 ish mahk

➕

`English` **dancing.**

`German` tanzen.

`Say It!` 🐱 TAHN-tsun

Others give you the name for a person,
place, thing, or idea.

`English` spring

`German` Frühling

`Say It!` 🐱 FREW-ling

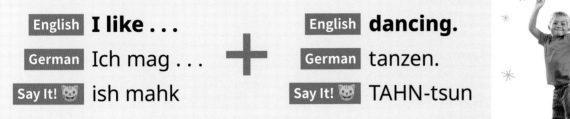

`English` milk

`German` Milch

`Say It!` 🐱 milsh

 Meet Chatty Cat! Chatty Cat will show you how
to say the words and phrases in this book.

Greetings and Phrases

German Grußformeln und Sätze

Say It! GROOS-for-meln
oont ZE-tsuh

English Hello!

German Hallo!

Say It! HAL-loh

English My name is . . .

German Mein Name ist . . .

Say It! mine NAH-meh ist

English What's your name?

German Wie heißt du?

Say It! vee haisst doo

English How are you?

German Wie geht es dir?

Say It! vee gate ess deer

English I am fine.

German Mir geht es gut.

Say It! meer gayt ess goot

English Nice to meet you.

German Schön, dich kennenzulernen.

Say It! shearn dish KEN-nen-tso-ler-nun

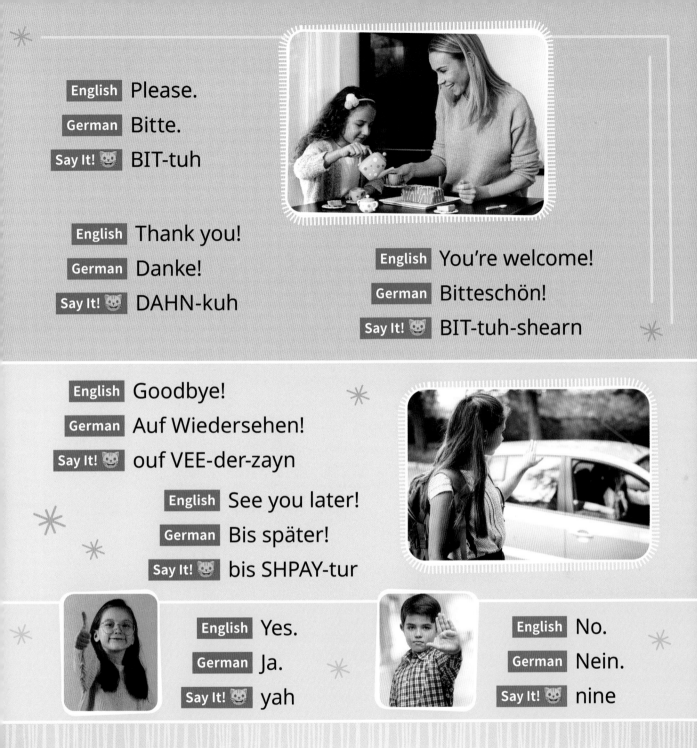

English Please.
German Bitte.
Say It! 🐱 BIT-tuh

English Thank you!
German Danke!
Say It! 🐱 DAHN-kuh

English You're welcome!
German Bitteschön!
Say It! 🐱 BIT-tuh-shearn

English Goodbye!
German Auf Wiedersehen!
Say It! 🐱 ouf VEE-der-zayn

English See you later!
German Bis später!
Say It! 🐱 bis SHPAY-tur

English Yes.
German Ja.
Say It! 🐱 yah

English No.
German Nein.
Say It! 🐱 nine

There is a unique consonant in the German language, the ß. It is called *eszett* (ehs-TSET). This letter always follows a vowel or vowel combination, like *eu*, *ei*, and *au*. It sounds like an *s*.

Family

German Familie
Say It! 🐱 fa-MEEL-ih-uh

English **This is . . .**
German Das ist . . .
Say It! 🐱 dahs ist

English These are my siblings.
German Das sind meine Geschwister.
Say It! 🐱 dahs zint MINE-uh guh-SHVIS-ter

English **my brother.**
German mein Bruder.
Say It! 🐱 mine BROO-der

English **my sister.**
German meine Schwester.
Say It! 🐱 MINE-uh SHVES-ter

English **my father.**
German mein Vater.
Say It! 🐱 mine FAH-ter

English **my mother.**
German meine Mutter.
Say It! 🐱 MINE-uh MU-ter

English **my aunt.**
German meine Tante.
Say It! MINE-uh TAHN-tuh

English **my uncle.**
German mein Onkel.
Say It! mine OHN-kuhl

English **my cousin.**
German mein Cousin. (boy)
Say It! mine koo-ZENG
German meine Cousine. (girl)
Say It! MINE-uh koo-ZEE-nuh

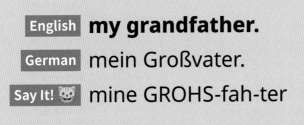

English **my grandfather.**
German mein Großvater.
Say It! mine GROHS-fah-ter

English **my grandmother.**
German meine Großmutter.
Say It! MINE-uh GROHS-mu-ter

In German, all nouns are capitalized.

Food

German Essen
Say It! 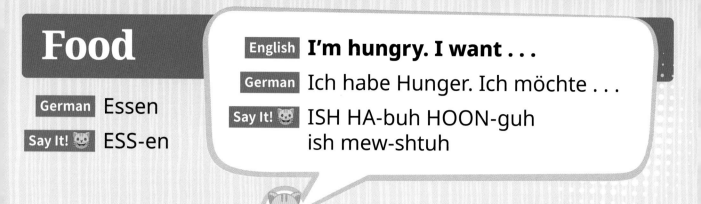 ESS-en

English I'm hungry. I want . . .
German Ich habe Hunger. Ich möchte . . .
Say It! ISH HA-buh HOON-guh
ish mew-shtuh

English to eat breakfast.
German frühstücken.
Say It! FREW-shtew-ken

English a bread roll
German ein Brötchen
Say It! ine BREWT-shen

English jam
German Marmelade
Say It! mar-meh-LAH-duh

English lunch.
German zu Mittag essen.
Say It! tsoo MIT-uhk ESS-en

English potato pancakes
German Kartoffelpuffer
Say It! car-TOF-fel-poo-fer

English a breaded cutlet
German ein Schnitzel
Say It! ine SHNIT-sel

English **dinner.**

German zu Abend essen.

Say It! 🐱 tsoo AH-bent ESS-en

English potato salad

German Kartoffelsalat

Say It! 🐱 car-TOF-fel-zah-laht

English a sausage

German ein Würstchen

Say It! 🐱 ine VURST-shen

English **a snack.**

German ein Snack.

Say It! 🐱 ine snek

English milk

German Milch

Say It! 🐱 milsh

English bread

German Brot

Say It! 🐱 broht

English an apple

German ein Apfel

Say It! 🐱 ine AHP-fel

English a cucumber

German eine Gurke

Say It! 🐱 I-nuh GOOR-kuh

Animals

German Tiere

Say It! 🐱 TEE-ruh

English a chicken

German ein Huhn

Say It! 🐱 ine hoon

English a dog

German ein Hund

Say It! 🐱 ine hoont

English a horse

German ein Pferd

Say It! 🐱 ine pfayrd

English a cat

German eine Katze

Say It! 🐱 I-nuh CUT-suh

English a fish
German ein Fisch
Say It! 🐱 ine fish

English a bird
German ein Vogel
Say It! 🐱 ine FOH-gul

English a pig
German ein Schwein
Say It! 🐱 ine shvine

English a frog
German ein Frosch
Say It! 🐱 ine frosh

English a cow
German eine Kuh
Say It! 🐱 I-nuh koo

13

At Home

German Zuhause
Say It! 🐱 tsuh-HOW-zuh

English a kitchen
German eine Küche
Say It! 🐱 I-nuh KEW-shuh

English a table
German ein Tisch
Say It! 🐱 ine tish

English a chair
German ein Stuhl
Say It! 🐱 ine shtool

English a living room
German ein Wohnzimmer
Say It! 🐱 ine VOHN-tsim-mer

English a computer
German ein Computer
Say It! 🐱 ine kom-PYOO-tuh

English a window
German ein Fenster
Say It! 🐱 ine FENS-ter

English a couch
German eine Couch
Say It! 🐱 I-nuh couch

English a bedroom
German ein Schlafzimmer
Say It! 🐱 ine SHLAF-tsim-mer

English a bed
German ein Bett
Say It! 🐱 ine bet

English a cell phone
German ein Handy
Say It! 🐱 ine HAN-dee

English a door
German eine Tür
Say It! 🐱 I-nuh tewr

English a bathroom
German ein Badezimmer
Say It! 🐱 ine BAH-duh-tsim-mer

English a sink
German ein Waschbecken
Say It! 🐱 ine VAHSH-back-uhn

English a toilet
German eine Toilette
Say It! 🐱 I-nuh toh-ah-LET-tuh

English a bathtub
German eine Badewanne
Say It! 🐱 I-nuh BAH-duh-vahn-nuh

15

Clothing

German Kleidung

Say It! 🐱 KLY-duhng

English **I am wearing . . .**

German Ich trage . . .

Say It! 🐱 ish TRAH-guh

English **a shirt.**

German ein Hemd.

Say It! 🐱 ine hemt

English **pants.**

German Hosen.

Say It! 🐱 HOH-zen

English **a hat.**

German eine Mütze.

Say It! 🐱 I-nuh MEW-tsuh

English **a coat.**

German eine Jacke.

Say It! 🐱 I-nuh YAHK-kuh

English **a skirt.**
German ein Rock.
Say It! 🐱 ine rock

English **socks.**
German Socken.
Say It! 🐱 ZOK-ken

English **a dress.**
German ein Kleid.
Say It! 🐱 ine klyd

English **shoes.**
German Schuhe.
Say It! 🐱 SHOO-uh

English **a sweatshirt.**
German ein Sweatshirt.
Say It! 🐱 ine SUET-shirt

17

In the Neighborhood

German In der Nachbarschaft

Say It! 🐱 in dare NAKH-bar-shahft

English a house

German ein Haus

Say It! 🐱 ine hous

English an apartment building

German ein Wohnhaus

Say It! 🐱 ine VOHN-hous

English a post office

German eine Post

Say It! 🐱 I-nuh posst

English a park

German ein Park

Say It! 🐱 ine pahrk

English a school

German eine Schule

Say It! 🐱 I-nuh SHOO-luh

English a hospital

German ein Krankenhaus

Say It! 🐱 ine KRAHN-ken-hous

English a library

German eine Bibliothek

Say It! 🐱 I-nuh beeb-lee-oh-TAYK

English a bus stop

German eine Bushaltestelle

Say It! 🐱 I-nuh BOOS-hahlt-uh-shteh-luh

English a grocery store

German ein Lebensmittelladen

Say It! 🐱 ine LEH-buns-mit-tel-lah-dun

English a street

German eine Straße

Say It! 🐱 I-nuh SHTRAH-suh

Transportation

German Transport

Say It! 🐱 trahns-PORT

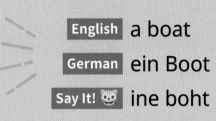

English a boat

German ein Boot

Say It! 🐱 ine boht

English a bus

German ein Bus

Say It! 🐱 ine boos

English a train

German ein Zug

Say It! 🐱 ine tsook

English an airplane
German ein Flugzeug
Say It! 🐱 ine FLOOG-tsoyk

English a truck
German ein LKW
Say It! 🐱 ine EL-kah-vay

English a car
German ein Auto
Say It! 🐱 ine OU-toh

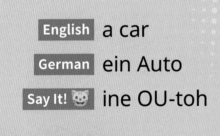

English a bicycle
German ein Fahrrad
Say It! 🐱 ine FAHR-rut

Automobiles and helicopters were invented in Germany.

Hobbies

German **Hobbys**
Say It! 🐱 HOHB-bees

English **I like . . .**
German Ich mag . . .
Say It! 🐱 ish mahk

English **singing.**
German singen.
Say It! 🐱 ZIN-gen

English **reading.**
German lesen.
Say It! 🐱 LEH-zen

English **painting.**
German malen.
Say It! 🐱 MAH-lun

English a book
German ein Buch
Say It! 🐱 ine bookh

English **dancing.**
German tanzen.
Say It! 🐱 TAHN-tsun

English **soccer.**
German Fußball.
Say It! 🐱 FOOS-bahl

English a ball
German ein Ball
Say It! 🐱 ine bahl

English **swimming.**
German schwimmen.
Say It! 🐱 SHVIM-men

English **bike riding.**
German Rad fahren.
Say It! 🐱 rut FAHR-un

Days of the Week

German Wochentage
Say It! 🐱 VOH-khen-tah-guh

English **Today is . . .**
German Heute ist . . .
Say It! 🐱 HOY-tuh ist

English **Monday.**
German Montag.
Say It! 🐱 MOHN-tahk

English **Tuesday.**
German Dienstag.
Say It! 🐱 DEENS-tahk

English **Wednesday.**
German Mittwoch.
Say It! 🐱 MIT-vukh

English **Thursday.**
German Donnerstag.
Say It! 🐱 DON-nas-tahk

English **Friday.**
German Freitag.
Say It! 🐱 FRY-tahk

English **Saturday.**
German Samstag.
Say It! 🐱 ZAMS-tahk

English **Sunday.**
German Sonntag.
Say It! 🐱 ZON-tahk

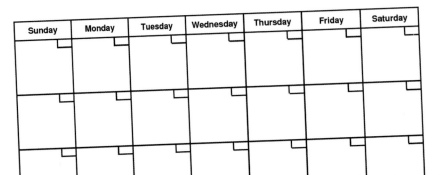

Seasons

English winter

German Winter

Say It! 🐱 VIN-tur

English spring

German Frühling

Say It! 🐱 FREW-ling

English summer

German Sommer

Say It! 🐱 ZOM-mehr

English fall

German Herbst

Say It! 🐱 hairpst

25

Weather

German Wetter
Say It! 🐱 VET-tur

English It . . .
German Es . . .
Say It! 🐱 ess

English **is raining.**
German regnet.
Say It! 🐱 RAYG-nut

English **is windy.**
German ist windig.
Say It! 🐱 ist VIN-dish

English **is cold.**
German ist kalt.
Say It! 🐱 ist cult

English **is snowing.**
German schneit.
Say It! 🐱 shnyet

English **is cloudy.**

German ist bewölkt.

Say It! 🐱 ist bev-EWLKT

English **is sunny.**

German ist sonnig.

Say It! 🐱 ist ZON-nish

English **is hot.**

German ist heiß.

Say It! 🐱 ist haiss

Colors

German Farben

Say It! 🐱 FAHR-ben

English red

German rot

Say It! 🐱 roht

English pink

German rosa

Say It! 🐱 ROH-zah

English green

German grün

Say It! 🐱 grewn

English orange

German orange

Say It! 🐱 or-AHNSH

28

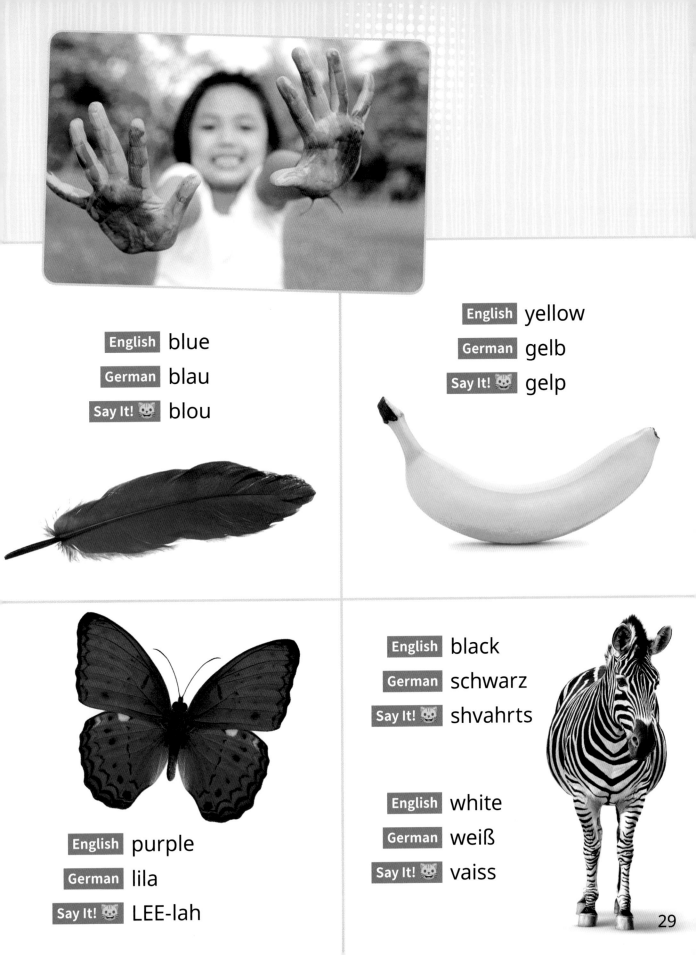

English blue
German blau
Say It! 🐱 blou

English yellow
German gelb
Say It! 🐱 gelp

English purple
German lila
Say It! 🐱 LEE-lah

English black
German schwarz
Say It! 🐱 shvahrts

English white
German weiß
Say It! 🐱 vaiss

29

Numbers

German **Zahlen**
Say It! 🐱 **TSAH-len**

1

English **one**
German **eins**
Say It! 🐱 **ains**

2

English **two**
German **zwei**
Say It! 🐱 **tsvai**

3

English **three**
German **drei**
Say It! 🐱 **drai**

4

English **four**
German **vier**
Say It! 🐱 **feer**

5

English **five**
German **fünf**
Say It! 🐱 **foonf**

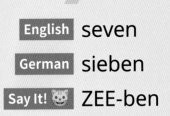

6

English	six
German	sechs
Say It! 🐱	zeks

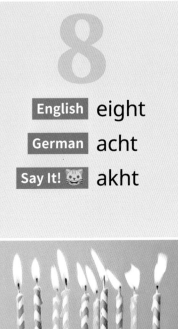

7

English	seven
German	sieben
Say It! 🐱	ZEE-ben

8

English	eight
German	acht
Say It! 🐱	akht

9

English	nine
German	neun
Say It! 🐱	noyn

10

English	ten
German	zehn
Say It! 🐱	tsehn

About the Translator

Monika Estrada is the Director of Language Education at the Germanic-American Institute in St. Paul, Minnesota. She grew up in Hamburg, Germany, and studied translation at the University of Leipzig. She is passionate about all aspects of language learning and especially enjoys watching children turn into multilinguals and use their skills in playful ways.